# THE BRUCE
# LEE WAY

# TIM BAKER
## FOREWORD BY SHANNON LEE

# TABLE OF CONTENTS

**W** **HEN I STARTED** looking after my father's legacy almost 20 years ago, I did so because I wanted people to understand the depth of the integrity of the soul that laid beneath the kung fu icon whose name everyone knew. Always looking for opportunities to share my father's life and philosophy with the world, I am pleased to be able to bring you this small encapsulation of some of his most meaningful life moments. My hope is this book will scratch below the surface of the name Bruce Lee to reveal to you the soul of an artist and a true warrior—fighting for what he most believed in while also pouring his creativity into the entirety of his life. These pages reveal my father as not just arguably the world's most famous martial artist, but also a poet, artist, writer, creator, thinker, innovator and human being.

Many people the world over have been inspired to undertake life changes and new directions for themselves because of my father's words and his impact. From professional athletes, artists and musicians to everyday people trying to live their best lives, my father's influence and reach continue to amaze and inspire me. As you encounter my father in these pages, I hope you too will be moved by the depth of his legacy. I am often told by people how my father's life, presence and words have helped give them hope and shape their experience in some way. It is always such a gift to me to hear how he's touched people's lives.

Bruce with his children Brandon and Shannon.

Even though I lost him when I was 4, my father's life has helped me through some very difficult times of my own. In particular, his urgings to actualize one's self rather than copying other successful personalities have helped me in the occasionally challenging position of being Bruce Lee's daughter. Whenever I feel like I have big shoes to fill or something monumental to live up to, his words remind me that the only monumental thing I have to live up to is my own life and no one else's. And I am reminded always how a person so focused on their own personal development, the expression of their soul out into the world and an attitude of brotherhood can—with their presence alone—create such a huge positive impact on the lives of so many. It encourages me to continue to be a beacon for this message so more and more people may discover for themselves, through the catalyst of Bruce Lee, to take up the path of their own evolution and positive connection with their fellow humans.

Maybe that's a lot to ask from a little Bruce Lee primer like this, but I encourage you to dig into some of the treasures that are found within these pages and see for yourself what wisdom and inspiration you can find. Perhaps this book encourages you to want to find out more about Bruce Lee and maybe even yourself! *The Bruce Lee Way* is really everyone's way in the end. So welcome to the journey, and thank you for bringing this book into your life along the way!

# —SHANNON LEE

# THE LIFE OF A DRAGON

## NOVEMBER 27, 1940

Lee Hoi Chuen and Grace Ho welcome their son Jun Fan Lee into the world at San Francisco's Jackson Street Hospital in Chinatown. A hospital nurse filling out the birth certificate suggests the English name of "Bruce."

## MAY 27, 1941

The Cantonese film *Golden Gate Girl* is released and features the on-screen debut of 3-month-old Bruce. The movie is the first Chinese-language film made in San Francisco.

## AUTUMN 1953

After enduring torment from bullies in school, a young Bruce starts studying martial arts under Yip Man, a master of the Wing Chun style of kung fu.

## APRIL 29– MAY 17, 1959

Bruce sets sail on an American Presidents steamboat to the United States after frequent altercations in Hong Kong lead his father to believe Bruce will be safer in the U.S. On the boat, Bruce teaches the first class passengers how to cha-cha.

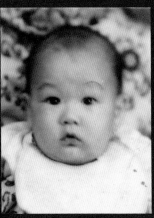

## MAY 27, 1961
Bruce enrolls at the University of Washington, where he meets his soon-to-be wife, Linda Emery.

# CHINESE GUNG FU
## The Philosophical Art of
## SELF-DEFENSE

by

### BRUCE LEE

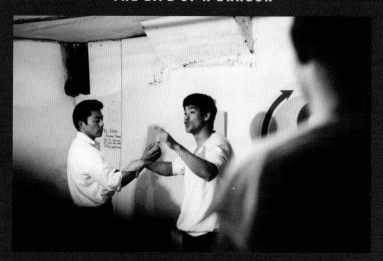

## JULY 19, 1964

After leaving the University of Washington, Bruce founds a kung fu school in Oakland, California, following the success of his first school in Seattle.

## AUGUST 17, 1964

Bruce marries his university sweetheart, Linda Emery. They go on to have two children together, Brandon (February 1, 1965) and Shannon (April 19, 1969).

## JUNE 6, 1966

*The Green Hornet* television series starts filming, starring Bruce as Kato. Despite its quick cancellation after only one season, the show helps set Bruce down a path to acting fame.

## JANUARY 8, 1967

The term "Jeet Kune Do" is first written down by Bruce to describe his style of martial arts, which combines elements of fencing, boxing and Wing Chun kung fu. He begins teaching the new style at his studio in Oakland.

## OCTOBER 23, 1971

The Hong Kong film *The Big Boss*, a kung fu movie starring Bruce, is released. The movie's huge success in Asia makes Bruce the face of kung fu cinema and leads him to make other classics in the genre such as *The Way of the Dragon* (1972) and *Enter the Dragon* (1973).

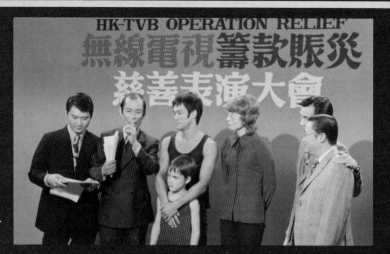

## JUNE 24, 1972

Bruce, Linda and Brandon Lee appear on the Hong Kong TVB *Operation Relief* telethon for victims of a typhoon that had recently devastated the area. Bruce also makes a personal contribution of $HK 10,000.

## JULY 20, 1973

During a busy day, Bruce lies down with a headache and never wakes again, passing away from a cerebral edema. His body is sent back to be buried by his wife in Seattle.

# REMEMBER YOUR ROOTS

HE MOST influential martial artist of all time came into the world in the year and the hour of the Dragon, November 27, 1940, between 6 and 8 a.m. In Chinese astrology, dragons are synonymous with dominance and ambition, known to streak across the sky with divine power at unmatchable speeds—much like the incomparable swiftness that would later characterize Bruce's famed fighting style.

Bruce as a boy in Hong Kong.

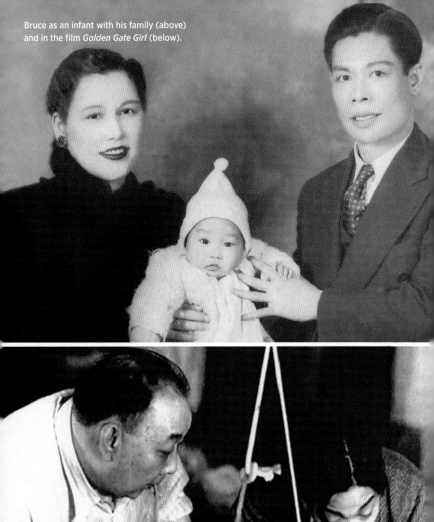

Bruce as an infant with his family (above) and in the film *Golden Gate Girl* (below).

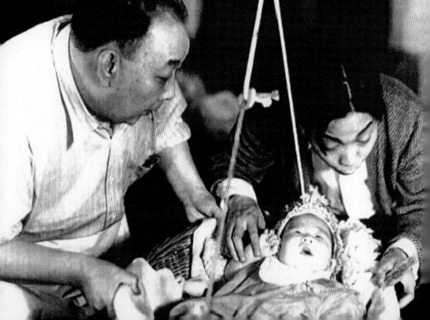

## REMEMBER YOUR ROOTS

The fourth child of Lee Hoi Chuen and Grace Ho, Bruce was born at Jackson Street Hospital in San Francisco, while his father was touring the States. But before he became Bruce, the English name a nurse gave him hours into his existence, his name was "Jun Fan." Bruce went by his Chinese name until he entered secondary school. At the time, his parents had no idea how indicative the original name—which roughly translates: "to arouse and make the United States prosperous"—would prove to be for the child who would become an icon responsible for instilling pride in Asian-Americans during a time when they were rarely portrayed positively in the media. Today, a plaque at the Chinatown hospital's entrance commemorates the birth of the 20th century's most significant martial artist and proves Bruce Lee, despite anecdotal evidence to the contrary, has always been human.

# LOOKING FOR INSPIRATION IN UNEXPECTED PLACES

S THE somber frugality of World War II slowly faded away in favor of the famed prosperity of the 1950s in the U.S., the citizens of New York, San Francisco, Honolulu, London, Hong Kong and scores of other cities were ready to enjoy a well-earned period of revelry. Films were shot in whimsical Technicolor, television was bringing a new kind of relaxation to the home and music was upbeat and made for dancing.

For much of the early '50s, the king of these dance steps was the mambo, imported from Cuba to the U.S. and able to spread all over the world thanks to its catchy syncopated

Bruce gives his younger brother Robert a dance lesson.

The young cha-cha expert shows off his moves.

## LOOKING FOR INSPIRATION IN UNEXPECTED PLACES

beat. But in the middle of the decade, experimenting bandleaders in Cuba ditched the syncopation of mambo in favor of a new style of subdivided beats borrowed from the rumba.

Bruce originally took up cha-cha with a close family friend named Pearl Tso as his partner before branching out to various competitions. With its focus on balance and precise footwork, in many ways the dance helped train Bruce for kung fu. Quick to realize this ancillary benefit of the nominally social activity, Bruce soon carried a notebook featuring more than 100 dance steps with him at all times to study. It wasn't long before Bruce was the Crown Colonies Cha-Cha champion and expert enough to instruct others—further proof of his commitment to applying himself fully to any task.

# LEARN FROM THE BEST

THE ORIGINS of Wing Chun are based in ancient Chinese legend, but its most famous practitioner is very much a real historical figure. In fact, his lifetime isn't so far removed from our own. As a boy, Bruce Lee was even able to learn from him directly. Considered the most brilliant practitioner in Wing Chun style's written history, Yip Man became an expert as a young man in Foshan, China.

An unimposing figure physically, Yip Man (pictured with Bruce) nevertheless commanded immense respect.

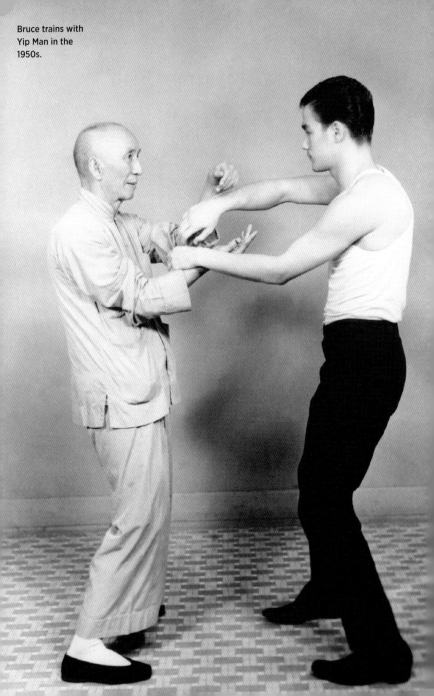

Bruce trains with
Yip Man in the
1950s.

At 12, Yip Man dropped out of school and began studying the ancient Wing Chun traditions with a local sifu, Chan Wah Shun, who initially tried to discourage the steadfast Yip Man by charging him vast sums of money for tutelage. But Yip Man would not be discouraged and began to love the graceful style of kung fu, in which posture is prized and the ideal form of both body and mind is likened to that of a piece of bamboo, firm but pliable.

By the time Bruce found a place under Yip Man's tutelage in the 1950s, Yip Man was renowned as the most graceful and powerful practitioner of his style. His students would later benefit from both of these traits. Yip Man's style and technique have been dramatized in films and on TV with regularity. It is these cinematic depictions, as well as his status as Bruce Lee's sifu, that constitute Yip Man's legacy today.

# KNOW THAT MISTAKES ARE ALSO OPPORTUNITIES

RUCE LEE famously practiced by throwing thousands of punches a day as an adult, but as a youth in Hong Kong, there wasn't always a regimen behind every blow. In fact, the Hong Kong high school boxing champion was involved with a street gang known as the "Junction Street Tigers." As a member, the young martial artist refused to back down from a fight with the son of a powerful gang member—one who had connections with the dangerous and ancient Triads—which put him in a dangerous situation.

In the midst of this possible danger, Bruce's father, Lee Hoi Chuen, made a decision that would change his son's life, sending his son back to San Francisco, the city of his birth. Here, it was hoped, Bruce could live a safer, healthier life.

He couldn't have known that in sending away his son— who excelled at everything he tried from cha-cha to boxing— he would start Bruce on a path that would continue to involve fighting, albeit in a very different way. Bruce would no longer be throwing punches to prove his toughness among other teenage gangsters. He would become a scholar, a teacher and finally, a star.

Hong Kong,
1950s.

"A goal is not always meant to be reached, it often serves simply as something to aim at."

—BRUCE LEE

Bruce as a boy in Hong Kong.

# STAY ON THE MOVE

HEN TOO MANY of us hit the gym, we're looking to give ourselves something to show off. But when Bruce Lee went, he did so with the mind of an architect: form follows function. The value of a good workout for Bruce was in how it made execution outside the gym so much more effective. Without a bodybuilder's acute sense of each muscle in his arms, chest and core, for example, Bruce would never have been able to execute the one-inch punch so devastatingly.

California in the 1960s was the perfect place to learn bodybuilding from some

Bruce mid-workout.
He was known to
practice hundreds
of punches a day.

*Fundamental Exercises :-*

1).
   Exercises for strength :- a) basic strength
   (power) b) functional strength *power*

2).
   Exercises for speed :- a) Repitition of basic movements = technique

3).
   Exercises for timing & coordination - a) sparring
                                         b)

4).
   Exercise for flexibility :- a) leg  b) stretching

5).
   Exercise for endurance :- a) ~~sparring~~ muscular endur
                              b) running
                              (vascular) fitness)

6).
   Exercise for agility :- a) agility exercise with light weight
                           b) jumping with kick

7).
   Nutrition & rest :-

8) Exercise for basic fitness :
   1) stomach :- ① sit up  ② leg raise  ③ side
                 ④ twist  ⑤ isometric  a) lower
                                        b) side
   2) leg   :- ① squat  ② isometric squat  ③ ju
               squat (with weight)
   3) back  :- ① deadlift  ② forward & ways bend

Bruce's notes on fundamental
exercises for strength, speed, timing,
flexibility, endurance and agility.

of the pioneers of the modern sport. Studying and improving upon the techniques of these athletes gave Bruce a foundation that eventually saw him add 35 pounds of muscle to his frame. But with what he felt was too much heavy muscle weighing down his speed, Bruce cut 20 of those new pounds down through cardio and attained the physique that would become famous on-screen.

Working out every day—Bruce used the technique of "active recovery" by engaging in intensive cardio on off-days from strength training—can become monotonous, but he knew complacency was an enemy of the kind of real-world strength and awareness he hoped to build. As he said himself: "There are no limits. There are only plateaus, and you must not stay there, you must go beyond them."

Linda.

To live content with
small means; to seek
elegance rather than
luxury, and refinement
rather than fashion, to
be worthy, not respectable,
and wealthy, not rich; to
study hard, think quietly,
talk gently, act frankly;
to bear all cheerfully,
do all bravely, await
occasions, hurry never.
In other word, to let
the spiritual, unbidden
and unconscious, grow
up through the common

Bruce
Oct 20 1963

# RECOGNIZE WHAT YOU LOVE

MANY OF Bruce Lee's lessons seem introspective, even stoic. But we can also learn from his loving and open nature, which he was never afraid to share. During the late summer of 1963, he was introduced to Linda Emery, a friend of one of his students, Sue Ann Kay. Kay had suggested Linda come along for a class, and before long the freshman at University of Washington was a regular student. Running into each other after a lesson one day, the two recognized their chemistry and agreed to go out on a date. Linda and Bruce would eventually marry and remain together until his death. Their relationship was marked by a characteristic openness from Bruce, reflected in the note included here. Just a few weeks into their relationship, Bruce described what he thought love should be like to the woman he was obviously already falling for.

Bruce and Linda Lee.

# MAKE YOUR OWN PATH

 RUCE LEE was famously against becoming too attached to any one discipline of martial arts, preferring to constantly learn and adapt new knowledge into his own unique style, the "style of having no style." Bruce was so committed to the idea of not being limited by the traditions of particular schools of martial arts that he even once staged a funeral with his own students for "the once-fluid man, crammed and distorted by the classical mess."

Bruce stands still, except for the blur of his right lower leg, mid-kick, as he gives a lesson.

Bruce spars with a
student as the rest
of his Jeet Kune Do
class watches.

According to biographer Bruce Thomas in *Bruce Lee: Fighting Spirit*, Bruce Lee "had assimilated as much knowledge and experience as he could about every aspect of fighting that he could use. He had amassed an extensive library, paying as much as $400 for a rare book" in the 1960s. As long as a book had something to do with fighting, Bruce bought it. He also meticulously studied films of boxing champions like Joe Louis, Rocky Marciano, Max Baer, Muhammad Ali, Jack Dempsey and other greats.

Bruce used the obsessive knowledge he gained of classical styles like boxing, karate, fencing and Wing Chun to create the art of Jeet Kune Do. Its philosophy was the same as Bruce's: learn from all, but become mired in none.

# SEIZE YOUR MOMENTS

 HAD SEEN IT ALL until I saw Bruce Lee perform with his philosophies, his concepts of martial arts and his speed and power," said Richard Bustillo, an eventual student of Bruce's, in an interview with the *Long Beach Press-Telegram* in 2014, speaking about the first time he saw the legend at work. "I said, 'Now this is something we have to learn. This is real martial arts.'"

Before Bruce demonstrated his skills at the 1964 Long Beach International Karate Championships, few in America

Bruce demonstrates the one-inch punch in Long Beach, California.

had seen the power and grace of Chinese martial arts. Westerners were much more familiar with the Japanese and Korean martial arts their contemporaries had brought home from military service in Asia, if they were familiar at all. But that was about to change.

This spike in interest was in part due to Bruce's unbelievable feats of strength, which included two-finger push-ups and his famous one-inch punch that sent a volunteer sprawling across the ring. But his charismatic presentation and willingness to question the status quo elevated his profile in the Bay Area, which in turn led him to a new aim: sharing his craft on film.

# 克 強 健 力 學 院
# HAK KEUNG GYMNASIUM

運動程序
### Exercise List.

繳費日期

學生姓名　　　性別

Name **BRUCE LEE** Sex **M** Date **MAY 27** 1965.

| | 運動名稱<br>EXERCISE | 組數<br>SETS | 磅<br>LBS | 次數<br>TIMES | 運動名稱<br>EXERCISE | |
|---|---|---|---|---|---|---|
| 1 | SQUAT | 3 | 95 | 10 | SQUAT | |
| 2 | FRENCH PRESS 1 | 4 | 64 | 6 | FRENCH PRESS | TRICEPS |
| | INCLINE CURL | 4 | 35 | 6 | FRENCH PRESS | |
| 3 | FRENCH PRESS 2 | 4 | 64 | 6 | PUSH UP | |
| | "CON" CURL | 4 | 35 | 6 | TRICEP STRETCH | |
| 4 | PUSH UP | 3 | 70-80 | 10 | INCLINE CURL | BICEPS |
| | TWO HAND CURL | 3 | 70-80 | 8 | "CON" CURL | |
| 5 | TRICEP STRETCH | 3 | 3 | 8(6) | TWO HAND CURL | |
| 6 | DUMBELL CIRCLE | 4 | 16 | INF. | REVERSE CURL | FOREARMS |
| | REVERSE CURL | 4 | X64 | 6 | DUMBELL CIRCLE | |
| 7 | WRIST CURL 1 | 4 | 64 | INF | WRIST CURL | |
| | WRIST CURL 2 | 4 | 10 | INF | WRIST CURL | |
| | | | | | | |
| | SIT UP | 5 | B.W. | 12 | SIT UP | |
| | CALF RAISE | 5 | B.W. | 20 | CALF RAISE | |

此表請勿攜出院外 Please do not take it away

# WORK (AND WORK OUT) WITH A PLAN

**IN 1965, BRUCE LEE** began an exercise regimen at the Hak Keung Gymnasium. The sessions there were intense even for someone used to an immense amount of physical activity, and exercises like the following three helped the young dragon indulge his bodybuilding phase with meticulous care.

**1 SQUAT** Best known as a useful leg exercise, squats also help create an anabolic environment—a physical state in which humans build muscle rather than creating energy by atrophy. This means that squats can actually help you build muscle all over. Bruce did three sets of 10 with 95 pounds of weight.

**2 WEIGHTED PUSH-UP** Body weight push-ups are among the most useful exercises for upper body and core strength, and adding weight is an expert move that makes them an exponentially more powerful tool. Proper placement of the weight near the center of gravity is essential, however, for avoiding injury.

**3 DUMBBELL CIRCLE** To work on his deltoids, Bruce would start with dumbbells at his sides and, keeping his arms straight, bring them up in front of him, then spread his arms out straight before returning to the original position.

# PASS IT ON

T EAST OAKLAND HOSPITAL on February 1, 1965, Bruce and Linda's son Brandon was born. Though Brandon admitted that other kids were afraid to come over because of the constant sounds of combat in the yard, Bruce was anything but an imposing father figure. His philosophy of being "like water" extended to fatherhood. A strong source of support and guidance, he also went out of his way to never be unyielding or needlessly hard. According to Linda Lee Cadwell on *The Bruce Lee Podcast*, Bruce considered fatherhood to be among his greatest achievements.

Bruce and Brandon at home in California.

Bruce Lee and
Van Williams
as Kato and the
Green Hornet.

# MAKE
# YOUR MARK

*REEN HORNET* was a beloved comic book and radio show by the time it was made into a television series in 1966, but it would be Bruce Lee's character from this series that would make the superhero a household name. Kato, the Green Hornet's sidekick, was always part of the comic's popularity, but on TV, Bruce was able to give the kung fu–fighting valet the charm and charisma that would eventually bring him to the big screen, and he fought for his own interpretation of the character's skill set. The gig on *The Green Hornet* only lasted one season, but it solidified Bruce's Hollywood ambition, as well as gave him a foot in the small-screen door.

Bruce threatens to make a decisive end to a foe in *Fist of Fury.*

"If you don't want to slip up tomorrow, speak the truth today."
—BRUCE LEE

Taky,

Just got back from the sporting good store — the special headgear they have on sale are all sold out. However, I did find out about those gloves and you can send a check of $15 to Dan Inosanto and he will get it for you — 212 Palos Verdes Blvd. Redondo Beach, Cal. 90277 As for the headgear, buy a regular boxing head-gear (enclosed you will find some sample from Ring magazine); it will be sufficient.

How's the class coming along? I'm sure everything will smooth out and shape up better and better.

I'm doing a Batman now — the Green Hornet and Kato will be the guest heros. I'm going to fight with Robin and we are supposed to come out 50/50 even and it's going to be a pain in the neck — that slow awkward double of his!

The Hornet series stopped shooting and will wait till April to find out whether or not we will be on for next year — as an hour.

Take Care my friend

Bruce

# KEEP IN TOUCH

TAKY KIMURA, Japanese-American martial artist and Jun Fan Gung Fu instructor certified by Bruce Lee himself, was also one of the most important people in Bruce's life. The best man at his wedding and Bruce's top student, Taky was one of the earliest acolytes of Jeet Kune Do. In the pictured letter, Bruce writes to Taky about some housekeeping matters for the school and informs his friend that Kato and the Green Hornet will be appearing on *Batman* as guest heroes.

Bruce was constantly writing down the philosophical musings that came to him, saving them for later use. Examples are all over this book. What came after was often another act of writing, with Bruce honing his original thought into a note or letter that he hoped would inspire students, friends or loved ones. This short note—almost a poem—to Taky Kimura focuses on another one of his motivating maxims: the power of positivity. In both letters, the point is proven that keeping in touch can be more than just reaching out—it can be creating life lessons and valuable memories.

To Taky Kimura

If You think you're beaten you are,
If you think you dare not, you don't,
If you like toukin but you think you can't,
It is almost certain you won't.

If you think you'll lose, you're lost,
For out of the world we find,
SUCCESS BEGINS WITH A FELLOW'S WILL——
Its all in the state of mind.

If You think You're outclassed, you are,
You've got to think high to rise,
You've got to be sure of yourself before
You can ever win a prize

Life's battles don't always go to
the stronger or faster man,
But sooner or later the man
who wins is the man
who thinks he can!

Bruce

# KNOW YOUR LESSON PLAN

**BRUCE WAS** often putting pen to paper, explaining his philosophy about Jeet Kune Do, or general thoughts on life, organizing and sharing principles like the following.

**HARMONY** Bruce aimed to constantly seek connection rather than opposition, making sure comparison of the self to others was a trap he'd never fall into. Being aware of one's surroundings and accepting them helps one act and react in harmony with both oneself and with the world.

**PEACE OF MIND** "All in all, the goal of my planning and doing is to find the true meaning in life—peace of mind," Bruce once said. But this doesn't mean being removed or aloof from everyday life, but rather accepting it, making it a harmonious part of yourself and calmly moving through the challenges life sends your way.

**SELF-CULTIVATION** Bruce's philosophy saw a person moving through three stages on their way to a cultivated self: Partiality, Fluidity and Emptiness. In the first stage, we are compartmentalized and defined by extremes. In the second, we are able to take what happens in the moment, relating and analyzing as we do so. In the third, we no longer need to analyze—we can let go of technique and simply respond.

Twentieth Century-Fox Television Inc.

BOX 900
BEVERLY HILLS, CALIFORNIA

George,

I've been shooting Batman these few days and busy like hell. I believe I should be able to find time to show your toy and his friends around the studio this coming Friday.

The Oklahoma appearance was great and I'm asked back for another one in Georgia. That sign you made has created quite a hit ~~ everyone admires your talents.

If you have time, I like to make two requests for some stuffs that you can make for me. They are gadgets to put my system across.

First, I like three signs ~~for hanging like picture on wall~~ ~~like pictures frames~~ ~~slightly smaller than the sign you made for me. Here are the plans & ideas ~~ this project by the way is to illustrate the thought behind my system ~~ the 3 stages

**1.**

**PARTIALITY**
THE RUNNING TO EXTREME

**2.**

**FLUIDITY**
THE TWO HALVES OF ONE WHOLE

Turn to save two

**3.**

EMPTINESS

THE FORMLESS FORM

Explanation for the three signs (same black shining background as the sign you made)

## FIRST SIGN

here all we need is one red half and one gold half of the Yin Yang symbol. HOWEVER <u>no</u> dot is need on either halves; in other word it is just plain red with no gold dot, or just plain gold with no red dot ( this serves to illustrate extreme softness (like 太极) or /and extreme hardness (like 达家). So just follow the drawing and also put the phrase — PARTIALITY — THE RUNNING TO EXTREME on the black board

## SECOND SIGN

Exact yin yang symbol like the sign you made for me except there is <u>no</u> chinese characters around the symbol. Of course, the phrase — FLUIDITY — THE TWO HALVES OF ONE WHOLE will be on the black board.

## THIRD SIGN

Just a shinny black board with nothing on it except the phrase EMPTINESS — THE FORMLESS FORM.

The three signs have to be the same size because they illustrate the three stages of cultivation. Please do make them like the sign you made for me aluminum and symbol and shinny black board

The second gadget I have in mind is used to dramatize the not too alive way of the Classical so called Kung Fu styles. miniature What I have in mind is a "tomb stone" and here is the drawing

IN MEMORY
OF
A ONCE FLUID MAN
CRAMMED AND DISTORTED
BY
THE CLASSICAL MESS

I'm sure you know how a grave looks like and make it with any material you like (aluminum tomb stone is fine) and at any size you want. Not too small though, because it's for display.

Call me collect if you have any problem
Thank you in anticipation   Bruce

The Art of Jeet Kune Do is simply to simplify.

Jeet Kune Do avoids the superficial, penetrates the complex, goes to the heart of the problem and pinpoints the key factors.

Jeet Kune Do does not beat around the bush. It does not take winding detours. It follows a straight line to the objective. Simplicity is the shortest distance between two points.

Jeet Kune Do favors formlessness so that it can assume all forms, and since Jeet Kune Do has no style, it can fit in with all styles. As a result, Jeet Kune Do utilizes all ways and is bound by none, and likewise uses any techniques or means which serves its end.

# NO STYLE IS THE BEST STYLE

**BRUCE LEE SAID, "Man is constantly growing, and when he is bound by a set pattern of ideas or 'Way' of doing things, that's when he stops growing."** More than any other principle, the idea that we must always be moving, adapting and bettering ourselves permeates his philosophy. For this reason, he eschewed any one style or tradition when devising Jeet Kune Do, seeing them as fetters that would keep students from striving toward self-improvement. In other words, complacency is the enemy of evolution, whether you're a martial artist or not.

# FREEDOM FIRST

**THERE ARE** words and phrases that come up more than once in Bruce Lee's philosophical writings, like "harmony," "effortless" and "self-actualizing." But finding any of these must follow achieving a sense of personal freedom. "Although I can tell you what is not freedom, I cannot tell you what is because that you must discover for yourself," Bruce said, and it's true that each person feels free in their own particular ways and settings. Finding a sense of being released from constraints is a key step in building mental strength, as it allows us to more confidently flow through life.

# JEET KUNE DO 截拳道

## PRIMARY FREEDOM :– a "frame" can kill the life of the situation by too rigid limitation

- \# Forms & prearranged sparring are means to shield oneself from facing reality in its suchness
- \# The "ISENESS" (FLUIDITY) is the primary freedom
- \# Dissolve like a thawing ice (it has form) into water (formless and capable to fit in with anything)
- \# When you have no form, you can be all form, when you have no style, you can fit in with any style
- \# In Primary Freedom one utilizes all ways and is bound by none, and likewise uses any technique or mean which serves its end.
- \# Enter a mould without being caged in it, obey the laws and principle without being bound by them.
- \# To be at an "undifferentiated center" of a circle that has no circumference
- \# Primary Freedom is the hinge of the pendulum which swings between the pro and con
- \# Not neutrality, not indifference but transcendence is the thing needed.
- \# The wheel revolves when it is not too tightly attached to the axle.
- \# With all the training thrown to the wind, with a mind perfectly unaware of its own

# BE OPEN TO LEARNING

**BRUCE LEE** might not have wanted to become attached to any one way of doing things, but he was always open to learning from established sources. For example, to modern readers, the yin-yang symbol is most instantly recognizable as a pop culture icon or a cliché tattoo. In ancient China, however, the yang side represented positivity, firmness, masculinity, substantiality, brightness, day and heat. The yin side represented negativity, softness, femininity, insubstantiality, darkness and cold. As Lao Tzu wrote in Book 1, Chapter 28 of the *Tao Te Ching*, of which Bruce kept a copy: "Know the masculine but keep to the feminine. And be a valley to the realm. If you are a valley to the realm, then constant virtue won't leave you...." In the following pages, Bruce offers his students a personal view of the ancient symbol's importance to kung fu.

<u>A brief explanation of our school emblem----the Yin/Yang symbol</u>

Instead of opposing force by force, a Gung Fu man completes his opponent's movement by 'accepting' his flow of energy as he aims it, and defeats him by 'borrowing' his own force. In order to reconcile oneself to the changing movements of the opponent, a Gung Fu man should first of all understand the true meaning of Yin/Yang, the basic structure of Chinese Gung Fu.

Gung Fu is based on the symbol of the Yin and Yang, a pair of mutually complementary and interdependent forces that act continuously, without cessation, in this universe. In the above symbol, the Yin and Yang are two interlocking parts of 'one whole', each containing within its confines the qualities of its complementaries. Etymologically the characters of Yin and Yang mean darkness and light. The ancient character of Yin (陰), the dark part of the circle, is a drawing of clouds and hill. Yin can represent anything in the universe as: negativeness, passiveness, gentleness, internal, insubstantiality, femaleness, moon, darkness, night, etc. The other complementary half of the circle is Yang (陽), which in its ancient form is written as (陽) or (昜). The lower part of the character signifies slanting sunrays, while the upper part represents the sun. Yang can represent anything as positiveness, activeness, firmness, external, substantiality, maleness, sun, brightness, day, etc. The common mistake of most martial artists is to identify these two forces, Yin and Yang, as dualistic (thus the so-called soft style and the firm style). Yin/ Yang is one inseparable force of one unceasing interplay of movement. They are conceived of as essentially one, or as two co-existing forces of one indivisible whole. They are neither cause and effect, but should be looked at as sound and echo, or light and shadow. If this 'oneness' is viewed as two separate entities, realization of the ultimate reality of Gung Fu won't be achieved. In reality things are 'whole' and cannot be separated into two parts. When I say the heat makes me perspire, the heat and perspiring are just one process as they are co-existent and the one could not exist but for the other. If a person riding a bicycle wishes to go somewhere, he cannot pump on both the pedals at the same time or not pumping on them at all. In order to go forward, he has to pump on one pedal and releases the other. So the movement of going forward requires this 'oneness' of pumping and releasing. Pumping is the result of releasing and vice versa, each being the cause and result of the other. Things do have their complementaries, and complementaries co-exist. Instead of mutually exclusive, they are mutually dependent and are a function each of the other.

My View On Gung Fu

Some instructors of martial art favor forms, the more complex and fancy the better. Some, on the other hand, are obsessed with super mental power (like Captain Marvel or Superman). Still some favor deformed hands and legs, and devote their time on fighting bricks, stones, boards, etc., etc.

To me the extraordinary aspect of Gung Fu lies in its simplicity. Gung Fu is simply the 'direct expression' of one's feeling with the minimum of movements and energy. Every movement is being so of itself without the artificialities which people tend to complicate it. The easy way is always the right way, and Gung Fu is nothing at all special; the closer to the true way of Gung Fu, the less wastage of expression there is.

Instead of facing combat in its suchness, quite a few systems of martial art accumulate 'fancy ness' that distort and cramp their practitioners and distract them from the actual reality of combat, which is 'simple' and 'direct' and 'non-classical'. Instead of going immediately to the heart of things, flowery forms and artificial techniques (organized despair!) are 'ritually practiced' to simulate actual combat. Thus, instead of 'being' in combat, these practitioners are idealistically 'doing' something about combat. Worse still, super mental this and spiritual that are ignorantly incorporated until these practitioners are drifting further and further into the distance of abstraction and mystery that what they do resemble anything from acrobatics to modern dancing but the actual reality of combat.

All these complexness are actually futile attempts to 'arrest' and 'fix' the ever changing movements in combat and to dissect and analyse them like a corpse. Real combat is not fixed and is very much 'alive'. Such means of practice (a form of paralysis) will only 'solidify' and 'condition' what was once fluid and alive. When you get off sophistication and what not and look at it 'realistically', these robots (practitioners that is) are blindly devoting to the systematic uselessness of practicing 'routines' or 'stunts' that lead to nowhere.

Gung Fu is to be looked through without fancy suits and matching ties, and it will remain a secret when we anxiously look for sophistication and deadly techniques. If there are really any secrets at all, they must have been missed by the seeking and striving of its practitioners (after all, how many ways there are to come in on an opponent without 'deviating too much from the natural course'?). True Gung Fu values the wonder of the ordinary and the cultivation of Gung Fu is not daily increase, but daily decrease. Being wise in Gung Fu does not mean adding more, but to be able to get off with ornamentation and be simply simple----like a sculptor building a statue not by adding but by hacking away the unessential so that the truth will be revealed unobstructed. In short, Gung Fu is satisfied with one's bare hand without the fancy decoration of colorful gloves which tend to hinder the natural function of the hand.

Art is the expression of the self. The more complicated and restrictive a method is, the lesser the opportunity for the expression of one's original sense of freedom! The techniques, though they play an important role in the early stage, should not be too restrictive, complex or mechanical. If we cling to

# JEET KUNE DO 武拳道
## (The 'Way' of The 'Stopping Fist')

### CHINESE BOXING
from the
### JUN FAN GUNG FU INSTITUTE

## Basic Defense

1. <u>Stop Hit</u> --- Jeet Da

   A. Back stop kick .......... Hou Jeet Tek
   B. Straight Stop Kick......... Jik Jeet Tek
   C. Hook Stop Kick ............ O'ou Jeet Tek
   D. Side Stop Kick............. Juk Jeet Tek
   E. Vertical Fist.............. Ch'ung Chuie
   F. Finger Jab................ Biu Jee

---

<u>NOTE:</u> In Jun Fan Gung Fu, there is no passive blocking. Instead of blocking a punch we usually use a stop hit to any place on the human body. A stop hit can be any kick or any punch.

---

2. Foot Obstruction, Stop Kick .... Jeet Tek

---

3. 4 Corners (Stop Hit with Parry)

   A. Right stop hit with high inside cover    Tan Da.

   B. Right stop hit with cross hand cover    Woang Pak Da

   C. Right stop hit with low inside cover    Loy Ha Pak Da

   D. Right stop hit with low outside cover    Ouy Ha Pak Da

---

| | |
|---|---|
| See Foo | Instructor |
| Sea Hing | Your senior, your older brother |
| Sea Dai | Your junior, your younger brother. |
| Sea Jo | Founder of the style and system |
| Sea Bak | Instructor's senior |
| See Sook | Instructor's Junior |
| Sea Gung | Grandfather, your instructor's instructor |

There are no limits. There are only plateaus, and you must not stay there, you must go beyond them."
—BRUCE LEE

Bruce and Van Williams practice martial arts moves for *The Green Hornet*

# BE LIKE WATER

"EMPTY YOUR MIND, BE FORMLESS. Shapeless, like water. If you put water into a cup, it becomes the cup. You put water into a bottle and it becomes the bottle. You put it in a teapot, it becomes the teapot. Now, water can flow or it can crash. Be water, my friend."

These sentences, perhaps the most famous of Bruce Lee's philosophical musings, are at once simple and all-encompassing. One only needs to watch him calmly move through a gauntlet

Bruce in *Enter the Dragon*.

Bruce reads *A Source Book in Chinese Philosophy* in his home library.

of a dozen opponents to know the words represent exactly how he hoped to move through life. The words are so much a part of Bruce's legend that it's easy to forget they were learned as part of a long and frustrating process beginning with his first kung fu lessons.

Studying with the famous Yip Man in Hong Kong, Bruce first heard about the mental side of martial arts when his teacher told him, "It's not just about punching and kicking, you need to flow with your opponent." But the esoteric lessons of martial arts had not yet penetrated. Eventually, Yip Man had had enough and told Bruce to go home for a week and think about what he'd been told over and over. Frustrated, Bruce took a boat into the harbor. With his hand trailing

behind him, grazing the surface of the water, he grew frustrated with his inability to take Yip Man's teaching to heart until, finally, he flailed out and struck the water violently with his fist.

This physical exhalation of frustration proved revelatory. When he lashed out at the water's surface, it naturally moved out of his way, consuming the blow and shifting around it. Trying to grab at the water and watching as it flowed through his fingers and back into the sea, Bruce realized water, though soft and supple, also carried with it great force. Water was the embodiment of the philosophy Yip Man had been espousing; both receptive and strong, smoothly moving and hard-striking.

Bruce rests in lotus position.

# STICK TO YOUR SCHEDULE

BRUCE LEE led a meticulous life: he was set on getting eight hours of sleep, dedicating time to playing with his kids, meditating, screenwriting, kung fu exercises, weight lifting, teaching and reading. Throughout his life, he also kept detailed diaries that helped him flesh out thoughts as they came to him.

RANDA                    JANUARY          1968

Holiday—Australia, Canada, New Zealand, Scotland, U.S.A.

MON.

| 9:20 - 9:30 | WARM UP (LEG-STOMACH) |
| 9:30 - 9:49 | RUNNING |
| 12 - 12:45 | PUNCH · 500 |
| | FINGER JAB - 300 |
| 3:00 → 3:55 | 1) Leg squat |
| | 2) leg stretching |
| | 1) pully |
| | 2) stand |
| | 3) Hook kick |
| | a) Left & right |
| | b) front & rear |
| 7:30 - 7:50 | FINGER JAB - 100 |
| | PUNCH — 200 |
| 9:00 - 9:30 | SIT UP — 4 SETS |
| | SIDE BEND — 4 SETS |
| TOTAL - 2 HRS. 59 min | LEG RAISE — 4 SETS |

**2**
**TUES.**

9:10 – 9:25   WARM UP
WAIST, LEG, STOMACH
9:27 – 9:41   RUN

11:30 – 12:35
PUNCH – 500
FINGER JAB – 400
3 PM – 3:45 – SQUAT
PUNCHING
   1) WEIGHT – 3 SETS
   2) LIGHT BAG – 20 MIN.
   3) HEAVY BAG – 3 SETS
   (EMPHASIZING LEFT CROSS)
5:15 – 5:45 – SIT UPS – 5 SETS
     SIDE BENDS – 5 SETS
     LEG RAISES – 5 SETS
8:20 – (4 min) FOREARM ISOM.

TOTAL : 2 HRS. 53 MIN.

CHUCK CALLED
(BLISTER ON FIST) NIGHT

---

**3**
**WED.**

Gung Fu workout – 7 – 9AM
stretching Hand (ALL DIRECTION)
9:00 – 9:15
WARM-UP – WAIST, LEG, STOMACH
9:20 – 9:50
PUNCH (BACK FIST) 500
SKIP ROPE – 3 SETS
10:00 – 10:30
FINGER JAB (500)
11:05 – 11:15   RUN
3:05 – 4:00
   1) HIGH KICK STRETCHING (L & R) 4 SETS
   2) SIDE LEG "   (L & R) 4 SETS
   3) PULLY HIP EXTENSION – 3 SETS
   4) RT. LEADING HOOK KICK
     1) heavy bag – 3 SETS
     2) paper – 3 SETS
   5) Rear left hook kick
     1) heavy bag – 3 SETS
4:15 – 4:35   2) paper – 3 SETS
STOMACH – WAIST – 3 & of 4 SETS
FOREARM ISOMETRIC

---

**4**
**THUR.**

10:35 – 10:45 – WARM UP
11:15 – 12:20 拳 (掌) 500
木樁 – 500 [詠春手樁]
12:53 – 1 O 2 (H) RUN
(Leo Called)
3:05 – 3:35 – PUNCHING
WEIGHT, PAPER, SKIP ROPE

:30 LOUPITTE OL 2-6750
8776 SUNSET BLVD.

:05 – 10:35
SIT UP — 4 sets
LEG RAISE — 4 sets
SIDE BENDS — 4 sets
FOREARM – WRIST ISOMETRIC

---

**5**
**FRI.**

9:10 – 9:25 – WARM UP
9:25 – 10:13 – PUNCH
(直中拳) – 500
木樁 – 500

CHUCK NORRIS – 11 a.m.
5 擒拿 手 practice

2:15 HAIRCUT APPOINTMENT

4:10 – 5 PM – LEG STRETCHING
PULLY & STAND (HIP)
STRAIGHT & SIDE
WORK ON LEFT SIDE KICK

8:30 — SIT-UP – 5 SETS
LEG RAISE – 5 SETS
SIDE BEND – 5 SETS
FOREARM – WRIST ISOMETRIC

LOUPITTE CALLED AT NOON
WROTE LETTER (REGISTERED)
TO BELASCO, THE GUILDE, DOZIER
SIGN CONTRACT WITH KENNARD

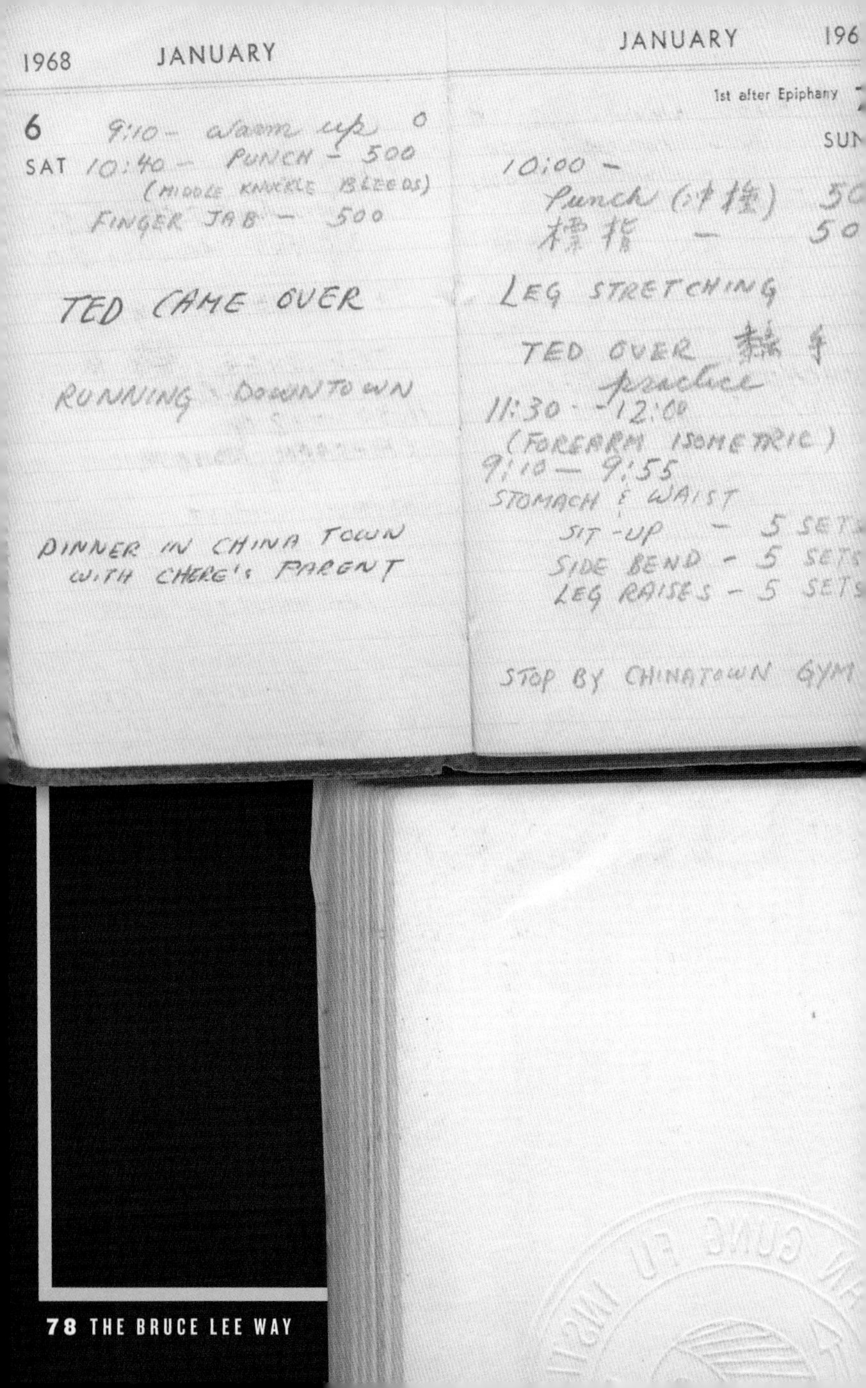

1968 JANUARY

6 SAT
9:10 – warm up
10:40 – PUNCH – 500
(MIDDLE KNUCKLE BLEEDS)
FINGER JAB – 500

TED CAME OVER

RUNNING DOWNTOWN

DINNER IN CHINA TOWN
WITH CHERE'S PARENT

JANUARY 196

1st after Epiphany
SUN

10:00 –
Punch (寸搥) 50
標指 – 50

LEG STRETCHING

TED OVER 黐手
practice
11:30 – 12:00
(FOREARM ISOMETRIC)
9:10 – 9:55
STOMACH & WAIST
SIT-UP – 5 SETS
SIDE BEND – 5 SETS
LEG RAISES – 5 SETS

STOP BY CHINATOWN GYM

# STICK TO YOUR SCHEDULE

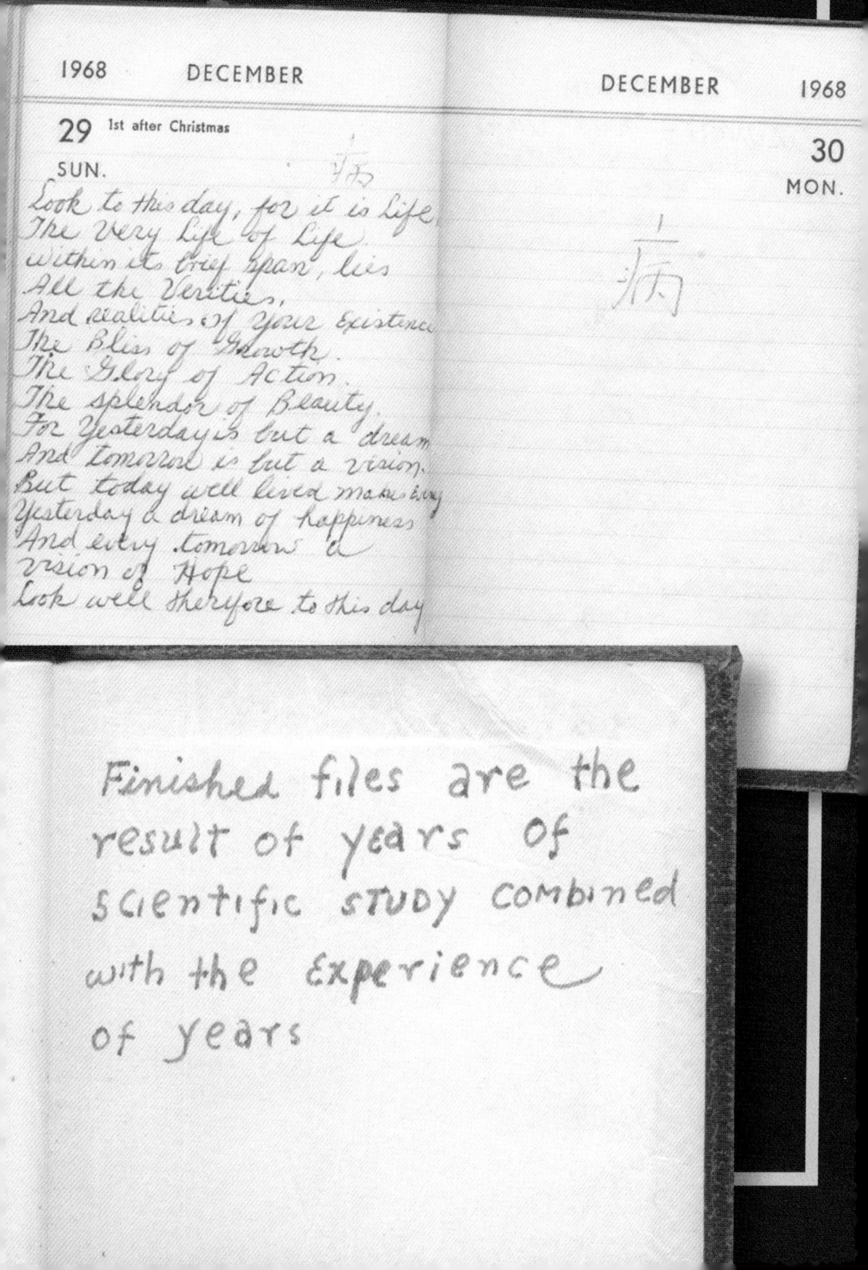

1968 DECEMBER

29 1st after Christmas

SUN.

病

Look to this day, for it is life,
The Very Life of Life
within its brief span, lies
All the Verities,
And realities of your Existence
The Bliss of Growth.
The Glory of Action.
The splendor of Beauty.
For Yesterday is but a dream
And tomorrow is but a vision.
But today well lived makes every
Yesterday a dream of happiness
And every tomorrow a
vision of Hope
Look well therefore to this day

DECEMBER 1968

30

MON.

病

Finished files are the
result of years of
scientific study combined
with the experience
of years

"Real living
is living for
others."
—BRUCE LEE

Bruce with his wife Linda and children Brandon and Shannon.

# KNOW YOUR GOALS (VERY) WELL

**AT THE BEGINNING OF 1969,** Bruce sat down and wrote a promise to himself. Beginning with "I, Bruce Lee," and listing his specific goals for the coming 1970s, the document reads almost like a contract. It's easy to imagine Bruce considering it a binding document, given the gravity of its wording and its level of detail. He even signs it like a contract and gives it a heading heavy with gravitas: "My Definite Chief Aim." If the first step toward achieving a goal is to visualize it, perhaps the second should be to commit pen to paper and sign on the dotted line.

# My Definite Chief Aim

I, Bruce Lee, will be the first highest paid Oriental super Star in the United States. In return I will give the most exciting performances and render the best of quality in the capacity of an actor. Starting 1970 I will achieve world fame and from then onward till the end of 1980 I will have in my possession $10,000,000. I will live the way I please and achieve inner harmony and happiness

Bruce Lee

Jan. 1969

# CARRY ALL OF YOUR STRENGTH WITH YOU

**TO HELP HIM** cultivate his mind as diligently as he worked on his physical fitness, Bruce Lee carried notecards with him at all times, each bearing an "affirmation." These clearly stated goals for mental cultivation and balance are just as valuable to aspirational individuals today as they were almost half a century ago when Bruce relied on them.

**WILL POWER** "Recognizing that the power of will is the supreme court over all other departments of my mind, I will exercise it daily when I need the urge to act for any purpose, and I will form habits designed to bring the power of my will into action at least once daily."

**EMOTION** "Realizing that my emotions are both positive and negative, I will form daily habits which will encourage the development of the positive emotions and aid me in converting the negative emotions into some form of useful action."

**REASON** "Recognizing that my positive and negative emotions may be dangerous if they are not guided to desirable ends, I will submit all my desires, aims and purposes to my faculty of reason, and I will be guided by it in giving expression to these."

## WILL POWER

Recognizing that the power of will is the supreme court over all other departments of my mind, I will exercise it daily, when I need the urge to action for any purpose; and I will form HABIT designed to bring the power of my will into action at least once daily.

## EMOTION

Realizing that my emotions are both POSITIVE and negative I will form daily HABITS which will ENCOURAGE the development of the POSITIVE EMOTIONS, and aid me in converting the negative emotions into some form of useful action.

## REASON

Recognizing that both my positive and negative emotions may be dangerous if they are not controlled and guided to desirable ends, I will submit all my desires, aims, and purposes to my faculty of reason, and I will be guided by it in giving expression to these

## IMAGINATION

Recognizing the need for sound plans and ideas for the attainment of my desires, I will develop my

imagination by calling upon it
daily for help in the formation
of my plans

## MEMORY

Recognizing the value of an
alert memory, I will encourage
mine to become alert by taking
care to impress it clearly with
all thoughts I wish to recall,
and by associating those thoughts
with related subjects which I
may call to mind frequently.

## SUBCONSCIOUS MIND

Recognizing the influence of my
subconscious mind over my power
of will, I shall take care to
SUBMIT to it a clear and definite
PICTURE OF MY MAJOR PURPOSE in life,
and all minor purposes leading
to my major purpose, and I
shall keep this PICTURE CONSTANTLY
BEFORE MY SUBCONSCIOUS MIND BY
REPEATING IT DAILY

## CONSCIENCE

Recognizing that my emotions often
err in their over-enthusiasm, and my
faculty of reason often is without the
warmth of feeling that is necessary to enable
me to combine justice with mercy in my
judgments, I will encourage my conscience to
guide me as to what is right or wrong, but
I will never set aside the verdicts it renders, no matter what may be the cost of carrying them

**IMAGINATION** "Recognizing the need for sound plans and ideas for the attainment of my desires. I will develop my imagination by calling upon it daily for help in the formation of my plans."

**MEMORY** "Recognizing the value of an alert mind and an alert memory, I will encourage mine to become alert by taking care to impress it clearly with all thoughts I wish to recall, and by associating those thoughts with related subjects which I may recall to mind frequently."

**THE SUBCONSCIOUS MIND** "Reorganizing the influence of my subconscious mind over my power of will, I shall take care to submit to it a clear and definite picture of my major purpose in life and all minor purposes leading to my major purpose, and I shall keep this picture constantly before my subconscious mind by repeating it daily."

**CONSCIENCE** "Recognizing that my emotions often err in their over-enthusiasm and my faculty of reason often is without the warmth of feeling that is necessary to enable me to combine justice with mercy in my judgments, I will encourage my conscience to guide me as to what is right and wrong, but I will never set aside the verdict it renders, no matter what may be the cost of carrying them out."

"The more we value things, the less we value ourselves."
—BRUCE LEE

Bruce in *Game of Death*.

# GROW WITH YOUR KIDS

**ECAUSE BRUCE** didn't have a traditional 9-to-5 job, he had the luxury of scheduling his days in such a way that there was always plenty of time to spend with his children playing, teaching and talking. When the Lee family welcomed Shannon on April 19, 1969, it meant Bruce felt this responsibility doubly. After breakfast and before dinner, Bruce took time every day to work on being a dad, just as hard as he worked at study and exercise.

Bruce and Shannon at home in California.

Bruce works
on his upper
body.

# NEVER
# SURRENDER

HEN BRUCE LEE injured his back during a routine training session in 1969, he was told by his doctor that the nerve damage was so severe he would never be able to perform martial arts again and perhaps never walk properly. Bruce immediately became a scholar about his specific type of injury, refusing to accept the devastating possibility that his life's work had been ruined by his failure to warm up for a single workout. Staying positive, he took an attitude that he later summarized in writing: "With every adversity comes a blessing because a shock acts as a reminder to oneself that we must not get stale in routine." Bruce slowly regained his strength with hard work and study, and he was eventually able to surpass his previous skills. For someone who cultivated his being as well as Bruce did, even an excruciating injury was an opportunity rather than a setback.

Bruce poses in front of the Jeet Kune Do symbol.

# ADD TO YOUR ARSENAL

HEN BRUCE LEE described his new style of martial arts, Jeet Kune Do, as "fencing without a sword," he wasn't just speaking with poetic license; he was describing a truth he had devised through intense study. Though we most often associate Bruce with Jeet Kune Do or his first style, Wing Chun, he was also a self-taught expert in many martial arts, including foil, épée and sabre fencing. He learned these western disciplines mostly through reading: his personal library contained more than 60 volumes on fencing theory alone. This level of dedication to a new way of thinking about martial arts is indicative of Bruce's idea of what Jeet Kune Do should be—an art form that draws strength from every new source it is introduced to while remaining independent. That's also exactly how he felt a person should seek to enrich themselves.

"I fear not the man who has practiced 10,000 kicks once, but the man who has practiced one kick 10,000 times."

—BRUCE LEE

| STUDENT NAME | | | | | | |
|---|---|---|---|---|---|---|
| | | | | | | 1-SUMMER |
| | | | | | | 2-AUTUMN |
| | | | | | | 3-WINTER |
| PERMANENT MEMBER NO. | SEX | RANK | YEAR | QTR | BRANCH | 4-SPRING |

## ~~ MEMBER ~~

### NOT TRANSFERABLE

## JUN FAN GUNG FU INSTITUTE

振 藩 國 術 館

THE UNDERSIGNED IS A REGULARLY ENROLLED STUDENT AT THE JUN FAN GUNG FU INSTITUTE FOR THE QUARTER AND YEAR INDICATED ABOVE.

SIGNATURE (NOT VALID UNLESS SIGNED IN INK)          (INSTRUCTOR)

CARD EXPIRES

MEMBERSHIP TERMINATES IF NOT RENEWED          (PRESIDENT)

## JUN FAN GUNG FU INSTITUTE

振 藩 國 術 館

*Using No Way As Way*
*Having No Limitation As Limitation*

# TAKE THE REINS

**WHEN BRUCE** founded his first martial arts school in Seattle, he was a young man, just finished with his time at the University of Washington, with only his own skill and knowledge to offer. There were other teachers with the benefit of more years of instruction or study, but Bruce was determined that no one would outwork him. Before long, his know-how and dedication had produced a legion of students (who carried cards like the one pictured), many of whom would one day become instructors and spread Bruce's teachings to a new generation.

# QUESTION YOURSELF

**WHEN BRUCE** was struck with a pertinent thought, his first instinct was often to write it down and extrapolate it. In this way, he was constantly probing the limits of his own mind and imagination in an effort to stay sharp. Much of the time, these thoughts would be about ways to better himself, questions to consider about his practice, or ideas for his teaching or his scripts. This note to himself, written on restaurant stationary, contains some of Bruce's thoughts on what it means to be an actor, from entertaining and educating the audience to becoming a part of the overall filmmaking process. Thinking about the nuts and bolts of his everyday actions and his long-term goals was one of the ways Bruce's mental strength helped him capitalize on all of his physical labor.

大 和 飯 店 （九 龍） 有 限 公 司

**RESTAURANT YAMATO (KOWLOON) LTD.**

ASHLEY BUILDING, 1st FLOOR, 14, ASHLEY ROAD,
KOWLOON

TEL. 3-674338
3-688323

What exactly is an actor?

An actor is, first of all, like you and me, a human being who, in this case happens to an artist. An artist capable of expressing oneself psychologically and physically with realism and appropriateness and, of course, hopefully in good taste. So what it really amount to is the revelation of a person's taste, his educational background, his early upbringing, learning, discovering (sometime much through the form of evoking, soul-searching or honest self inquiries) etc etc. Just as no two human beings are born alike, the same hold true for actors.

Film-making is basically a marriage of business and art, and in the eyes of the studio administrators or the money people an actor is often referred to as a saleable product, commodity, box-office holders, etc etc.

Why the difference —

Because you can, as human being, dedicate yourself and train so hard on what you can deliver; well, the money people will listen.

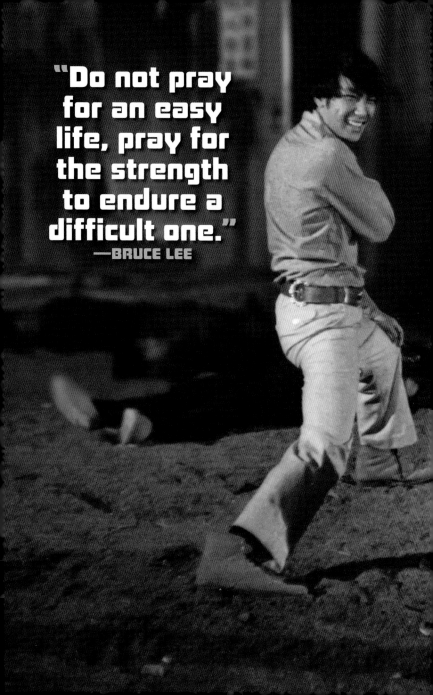

"Do not pray for an easy life, pray for the strength to endure a difficult one."

—BRUCE LEE

# WHEN YOU'VE GOT IT, SHOW IT OFF

IRECTED BY prolific Chinese filmmaker Lo Wei in 1971, *The Big Boss* (aka *Fists of Fury*) sees Bruce as Cheng Chao-an, a young Chinese man who moves to Pak Chong, Thailand, to live with his cousins. Prior to his departure, Cheng makes a promise to his mother to abstain from violence of any kind, an oath he keeps at the top of mind by wearing his mother's jade amulet necklace. Upon arrival in Pak Chong, Cheng's pacifism is tested by an encounter with local street thugs.

Once Cheng's fists start to fly, *The Big Boss*'s action unfolds with a ferocity that would become the signature cinematic style of Bruce's films to come. Wearing a white shirt and a white sash—the color traditionally used to symbolize death in

Bruce in *The Big Boss*. The film would go on to be Hong Kong's highest grossing for 1971.

Bruce as Cheng.
Although Ying-Chieh
Han was the official
fight coordinator,
Bruce was in charge
of his own scenes.

## WHEN YOU'VE GOT IT, SHOW IT OFF

Chinese culture—Cheng is fighting to kill. He initiates a battle by throwing a blade into the face of one of the foes, then alternates between swiftly stabbing and spin-kicking the men as they attempt to attack him. Despite being vastly outnumbered, Cheng outsmarts and outmaneuvers the gang as the fight progresses, dodging knife throws, delivering fatal blows and even sending a man crashing through a wall with a single punch.

Spanning just four minutes of screen time, the scene was a high-octane whirlwind and unlike anything that'd ever been committed to celluloid. It would, unquestionably, cement Bruce's place as a star, simply because no one had ever seen moves like these before. East and west alike were ravenous for Bruce Lee footage after *The Big Boss*, and his lifetime of hard work was beginning to make the kind of impact he had always hoped it would.

Bruce in *The Way of the Dragon*.

"Absorb what is useful. Reject what is useless. Add what is essentially your own."

—BRUCE LEE

# REVENGE IS BEST SERVED IN FICTION

EFORE HE MADE *Fist of Fury* (also released as *The Chinese Connection*), Bruce Lee was struggling to gain real traction in the movies. In Hong Kong, he was slightly well-known thanks to his role as Kato on *The Green Hornet*, but Bruce knew he was ready for more. *Fist of Fury* was the vehicle he needed, and Bruce made the most of the opportunity he knew he might not get again.

Bruce Thomas, in his biography *Bruce Lee: Fighting Spirit*, calls the 1972 film a "hymn of revenge," and it's easy to see why: The film's main conflict arises from the historical animosities between the people of China and Japan and is set at a time when the latter country took pleasure in describing China as the "Sick Man of Asia." *Fist of Fury*'s release brought with it strong feelings of Chinese national pride in Hong Kong—the city was,

Bruce as Chen Zhen fights his way through a Japanese dojo.

Chen Zhen squares off against a Russian wrestling champ and fights more adversaries.

unstoppable!
unbelievable!
unbeatable!

BRUCE LEE

The master of karate / kung fu is back
to break you up, smash you down
and kick you apart with

"THE CHINESE
CONNECTION"

## REVENGE IS BEST SERVED IN FICTION

after all, only 30 years removed from the horrors of Japanese fascism. Thomas compares it to "[the atmosphere] in England after the English football team beat Germany" in the 1966 World Cup final. "It wasn't simply a matter of winning a game of football," he continues, "just as what was happening on the streets of Hong Kong...was more than simple popular reaction to an exciting new movie. It was a matter of national pride, of triumph over a rival."

By bringing the story of Chen Zhen to the big screen, Bruce gained the kind of leading-man credentials he hoped would bring him global recognition. In its original month-long run in theaters, *Fist of Fury* performed like the star-making vehicle it was, breaking records and making more than HK$ 4 million at the box office. Scalpers outside of packed theaters were charging up to $50 for a single ticket, and before long, Bruce was unable to walk down the main street of the city without being mobbed by fans and admirers. Following the film's success, Run Run Shaw of Shaw Brothers, a former employer of Bruce's, attempted to lure him back from Golden Harvest Pictures with a blank check.

"Be happy, but never satisfied."
—BRUCE LEE

Bruce behind the scenes of *Enter the Dragon*.

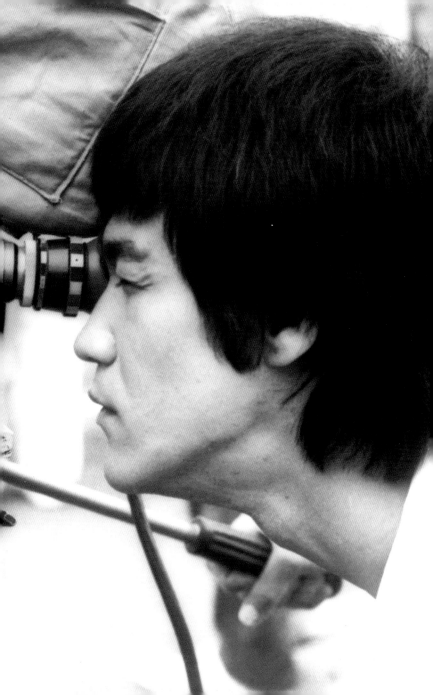

# NEVER DESPAIR

ITH TWO FILMS under his belt and a growing reputation in Asia as a bona fide star, Bruce Lee was hungry for a true crossover to Hollywood stardom. He may have appreciated the attention his early work had brought (the Hong Kong press had taken to calling him the "king" of that city), but he also felt his work ethic and level of skill by this time merited a place in the mainstream.

But at the end of 1971, this overall goal seemed somehow just as distant as it always had. In an interview with Canadian TV reporter Pierre Berton that year, Bruce expressed his frustration with the American moviemaking system. "I have already made up my mind that...something of the Oriental, I mean the true Oriental, should be shown," Bruce says. "Hollywood sure as heck hasn't," comes Berton's reply.

"You better believe it man," Bruce continues. "I mean, it's always the pigtail and the bouncing around, chop-chop, you know, with the eyes slanted and all that." His reply is telling: Even someone as strong-willed and

Bruce squares off against Chuck Norris in *The Way of the Dragon*.

From top: Bruce with Hong Kong film producer Raymond Chow; Bruce in a still from *The Way of the Dragon*.

strong-bodied as Bruce Lee could be hemmed in by ever-present systems of prejudice and discrimination.

But rather than become mired in these feelings, Bruce combatted their source by making exactly the right movie at the right time, going to Europe to prove that he could be just as impressive in a western context. In Italy, Bruce forged his own path rather than lamenting the racism of the Hollywood system, creating one of his most beloved films in the process.

*The Way of the Dragon* tells the story of Tang Lung, a rural Chinese man who leaves the country to meet distant relatives in Rome. Much of the early part of the film is played for laughs as Tang Lung fails to properly communicate his wants or needs in the strange city. He is soon met by his cousin, memorably portrayed by Nora Miao, who reveals the film's main conflict. After the seeming good fortune of inheriting a restaurant, she has discovered the mafia is interested in the land on which it sits. The laughs never stop—the film even contains well-timed pauses in dialogue to allow for audience reaction—but Bruce's earnest direction also includes crisp fight scenes and, as biographer Bruce Thomas puts it, some free kung fu lessons to boot. Bruce also showed, in his own way, how well a Chinese lead could play in a western setting.

Bruce with his son
Brandon in L.A.

"What you
habitually
think
largely
determines
what
you will
ultimately
become."
—BRUCE LEE

# INDULGE YOUR IMAGINATION

IT'S EASY TO THINK of Bruce Lee only in terms of his imposing martial skill, but cultivating that skill required more than just working out and sparring. Bruce knew an effective martial artist was a well-rounded and constantly evolving human being whose skills extended far beyond the violent. This is one of the reasons Bruce often took time to indulge his love of drawing. Bruce's personal notebooks are full of sketches—like this dragon imploring those who see it to "Think!"—and all of them performed a vital function in Bruce's development as a person: keeping his imagination as active and limber as the rest of him.

# FIGHT
# WITHOUT
# FIGHTING

N *ENTER THE DRAGON*, Bruce Lee's philosophy is just as much on display as his fighting skills, a trend he hoped to continue with *Game of Death* and his unfinished screenplay that would eventually be produced as *Circle of Iron* after his death. Given the amount of personal writings he left behind, had Bruce lived, it's easy to imagine a long series of films packed with jeet kune do technique as well as its philosophical underpinnings in amazing fight scenes. A perfect example is an early set piece in *Enter the Dragon* with which he would illustrate how a fighter could, with such a mind, flow around and through anything in their path.

From top:
Bruce in *Enter the
Dragon*'s Shaolin temple
scene; Bruce fights in
*Enter the Dragon*.

## FIGHT WITHOUT FIGHTING

When a brash combatant from New Zealand on his way to the martial arts tournament that makes up the setting for *Enter the Dragon* picks a fight with Bruce's character, the situation provides a chance to showcase an original Bruce Lee fable. The fable's moral could only be one thing: "Be like water, my friend." "What's your style?" the Kiwi asks, to which Bruce responds, "You could call it the art of fighting without fighting." When the westerner suggests a fight, Bruce's character suggests they take a lifeboat to a nearby beach to brawl. But when his nemesis is aboard the lifeboat, Bruce simply unmoors the craft and sets him out to sea. Faced with a blustering adversary not worth his time or energy so soon before such an important assignment, Bruce dispatches him without even breaking a sweat.

Bruce reflects in a garden.

"Remember no man is really defeated unless he is discouraged."
—BRUCE LEE

# MENTALLY STAGE YOUR SUCCESSES

SOMETIMES, after doing hard, intense thinking about a project—hours of scriptwriting for *Enter the Dragon*, for example—the best way to unwind is by doing some easy thinking as a cooldown. Bruce was an extremely talented sketch artist and often sketched out the way he felt fight scenes should look, executing the notoriously difficult limbs of martial artists, sometimes in elaborate costumes. But just as often, he was apt to use his drawing skills as a form of active meditation just as he used running. This "Enter the Dragon" dragon is likely the result of something like this process.

Enter The Dragon

# DON'T BE AFRAID TO BE RIGHT

CCORDING TO LINDA LEE CADWELL, Bruce's widow, on *The Bruce Lee Podcast*, making *Enter the Dragon* as good a movie as it turned out to be was a fight in itself: "This was the breakthrough. The Hollywood connection—his ticket back into Hollywood. He wanted to elevate the image of a Chinese person and introduce the audience to Chinese culture, which was 5,000 years old. Bruce Lee didn't invent martial arts movies...[but he] wanted to bring a little bit more depth in the movie and...show the beauty of Chinese culture and philosophy." So when the producers, writer, cast and crew arrived in Hong Kong expecting to begin shooting right away, Bruce had different ideas. "He didn't want to start shooting until the script was finished," continues Linda. But this wasn't the norm in a Hong Kong film industry that prized speed of production over quality, so when Bruce insisted they make edits to include some philosophical notes, Linda says the writer and producers weren't happy, but Bruce ultimately knew he could make the movie better.

Linda carries Shannon while Bruce and Brandon walk beside her in 1971.

# RESPECT THE TECHNIQUE

**DESPITE THE fact that while he was wrapping his *Game of Death* script and preparing to shoot *Enter the Dragon* Bruce was busier than he ever had been, he took the time to write a letter to himself which he called "In My Own Process." In fact, he went through seven drafts of the letter, two of which are pictured here, each of which fleshed out his main theme a bit more. Self-honesty and a constant quest for quality were at the forefront, but the main lesson to be learned is that Bruce was self-aware enough to realize exactly when a thought was too important to ignore.**

NOTES ON ARTICLE -

concentration — that which has a common center, it is
  to          moving toward a tender
awareness

Bruce Lee is a changing person because he is and
always will be learning, discovering and expanding. Like
his martial art, his learnings are never fixed. They
keep changing et but Bruce Lee presents a possible
direction but getting more and author fine, admire
some significants and to brighter attitude
traits of Bruce Lee are to honesty to oneself,
quality over quantity ( to put it in his word,
I can walk away million because it is no sign
but I 'damned if I back up an inch from a dame
all because it has to be so) last but nd least
he is a performer hard working man though
over 90% of superstar who can be in
his shoes, will be neglecting his worth
and abuse his power

In my own Process —— By Bruce Lee

Any attempts to write a somewhat "meaningful" article —— or else why write it at all —— on how I, known as Bruce Lee by name, emotionally feel or how my instinctive reaction toward circumstance is, no easy task. It all depends because what's true yesterday might not be so to-day. I'm sure, I'm changing

This article can very well be made less demanding should I indulge myself in the much practiced game of manipulating one's image. I am afraid My understanding as least can differentiate between self-actualization and self-image actualization. I know, I am most here to write any confession — but I am the type of man who takes responsibility to himself & will. I seems to be honest, you are not

To be a professional actor is the sum total of all that he is now spiritually, psychologically, physically, his experiences, his attitude, etc. etc. can go on and on. A true actor is one who can blend appropriately around of this twoneness of commercial creativity and creative commerce such artist actor is known creatively as a deliverer and to the business men, he is a good risk of his box office. I have an automatic toward admiration film-makers who devote themselves to the "quality" of making an out of sight film. A film, because everyone of this unit is pouring his heart and soul in it, is what make this a success. —— not just any one character.

# KNOW WHEN TO PULL OUT ALL THE STOPS

FTER TAKING the cinematic and martial arts worlds by storm in a few short years, Bruce Lee's tragic death left fans wondering if the kung fu renaissance he had helped start would die with him. *Game of Death* proved that not only was kung fu here to stay, Bruce would forever be its ambassador. He had worked on the idea for years, a film that he hoped would fuse his skills as an entertainer and a teacher to create something that both wowed and enriched the audience.

Envisioning a fable in which his character's brother and sister are kidnapped by Korean gangsters, Bruce set up a story in which his quest for revenge would span multiple fights with his most famous and skilled students and friends. Bruce's *Game of Death* would have

Bruce in his iconic yellow *Game of Death* jumpsuit.

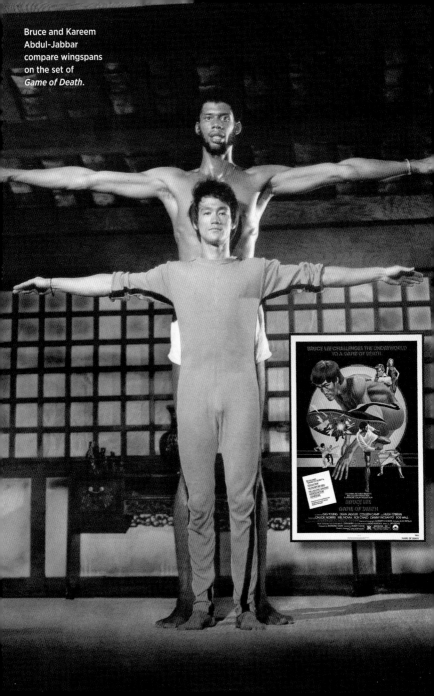

Bruce and Kareem Abdul-Jabbar compare wingspans on the set of *Game of Death*.

been a spectacle the likes of which kung fu cinema had never seen before. Bruce was so dedicated to his idea that he began filming some of *Game of Death* before making *Enter the Dragon*. His legendary fight scene with Kareem Abdul-Jabbar, for example, only exists today because of Bruce's dedication to his biggest project yet. Had he been less zealous about the film, the 40-odd minutes of footage he created before his passing wouldn't exist. There would be no Billy Lo, no iconic yellow jumpsuit, no Bruce vs. Kareem and no final Bruce Lee movie to enjoy. The scene sketches on the following spread are a perfect example of just how hard and how often Bruce thought about what would become his cinematic swan song.

The film that was eventually made by producer Raymond Chow and director Robert Clouse bears little resemblance to Bruce's original idea: The small amount of footage Bruce compiled was supplemented with cutting room floor scraps. These included pieces from his other films, scenes in which stand-ins played his role and also footage from Bruce's real-life funeral. But Bruce's dedication ensured that fans got one more movie with the Dragon.

PICTURE (A)

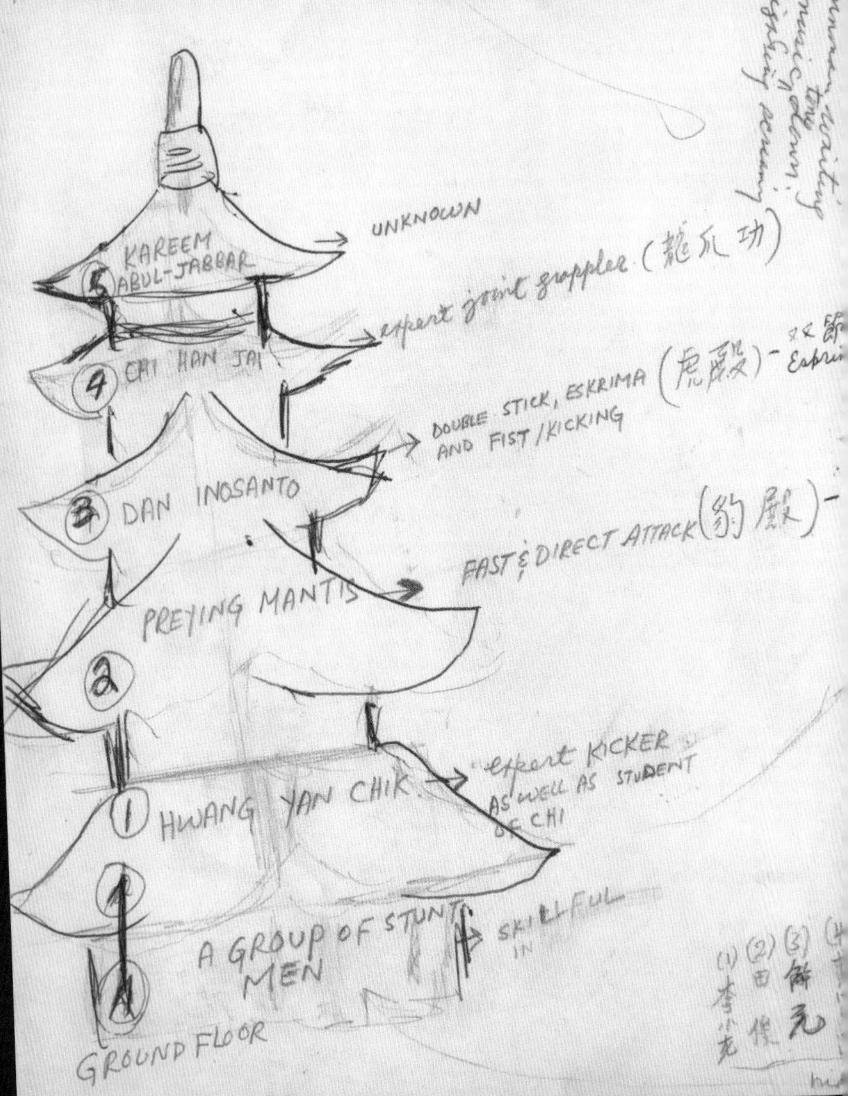

UNKNOWN

⑤ KAREEM ABUL-JABBAR — expert joint grappler (龍爪功)

④ CAI HAN JAI — DOUBLE STICK, ESKRIMA (虎殺) – Eskri

③ DAN INOSANTO — FAST & DIRECT ATTACK (豹殺) –

PREYING MANTIS

②

① HWANG YAN CHIK — expert KICKER AS WELL AS STUDENT OF CHI

A GROUP OF STUNT MEN — SKILLFUL IN

GROUND FLOOR

(1) 李小克
(2) 田俊
(3) 解元

WHEN IMAGINING *Game of Death*'s central premise, Bruce envisioned a six-part fight sequence that worked its way up the levels of a pagoda, with each floor featuring an opponent who would challenge his fighting style and force him to adjust his approach to battle.

**BRUCE EVEN** took the time to sketch what the exterior of *Game of Death*'s pagoda and the surrounding courtyard where the first of his six fights—against a group of guards—would have taken place.

PICTURE (B)

ATTACKING PLAN (

Bruce relaxes on set.

"Don't fear failure. Not failure, but low aim is the crime. In great attempts it is glorious even to fail.

—BRUCE LEE

The dying sun lies sadly in
the far horizon.
The autumn wind blows mercilessly
The yellow leaves fall.
From the mountain peak, two streams
parted unwillingly;
One to the west, one to the east.

The sun will rise in the morning.
The leaves will be green again
In spring.
But must we be like the
Mountain stream to part and
Never to meet again?

                              Bruce Lee

# FIND YOUR INNER POET

The dying sun lies sadly in
The far horizon
The autumn wind blows mercilessly.
The yellow leaves fall
From the mountain peak, two streams
parted unwillingly;
One to the west, one to the east.

The sun will rise in the morning,
The leaves will be green again
In spring
But must we be like the
Mountain stream to part and
Never to meet again?

BRUCE LEE

**Media Lab Books**
**For inquiries, call 646-838-6637**

Copyright 2019 Topix Media Lab

Published by Topix Media Lab
14 Wall Street, Suite 4B
New York, NY 10005

Printed in Hong Kong

ISBN-13: 978-1-948174-28-2
ISBN-10: 1-948174-28-6

BRUCE LEE and the Bruce Lee signature are registered or pending trademarks of Bruce Lee Enterprises, LLC in multiple countries. The Bruce Lee name, image, likeness and all related indicia are intellectual property of Bruce Lee Enterprises, LLC. All rights reserved. www.brucelee.com.

Special thanks to Bruce Lee Archivist **Jess Scott** for her research and expertise

All photos Bruce Lee Enterprises, LLC except: 11 AF Archive/Alamy; 27 Richard Harrington/Three Lions/Getty Images; 48 Silver Screen Collection/Getty Images; 68 Everett Collection; 106 Courtesy Heritage Auctions; 112 Courtesy Heritage Auctions; 118 Courtesy Heritage Auctions; 126 Courtesy Heritage Auctions; 138 Courtesy Heritage Auctions